The work of Reginald P. Phillimore

in old picture postcards

by
Donald Lindgren

European Library – Zaltbommel/Netherlands

Acknowledgement:
I wish to record my thanks to those who have helped me with information about Reginald P. Phillimore. It was fascinating to speak to those who remember him as he went with his sketch pad, around the area of North Berwick, making drawings for his delightful postcards. This book would not be possible without the kindness of Margaret K. Graham who so graciously allowed me to use, from her wonderful collection, most of the postcards illustrated in this book. I am thankful to my friend, George Smith MA, who has always encouraged me and made valuable suggestions as he has proof-read and corrected my text. And to Reginald Phillimore Phillimore himself, we are all grateful for providing such a rich treasure of charming drawings and fascinating historical notes on his unique series of postcards.

By the same author:
Musselburgh in old picture postcards volumes 1 and 2
The Firth of Forth in old picture postcards volumes 1 and 2

GB ISBN 90 288 5264 6 / CIP

INTRODUCTION

Collectors of postcards, particularly in Scotland, every once in a while come across an unusual and distinctive series of cards that are obviously drawings but often with relevant historical notes and related vignettes to compliment the scene drawn by the artist. These fascinating postcards are becoming rare and eagerly sought after by collectors. Many of them depict scenes around North Berwick and East Lothian but other beauty spots and historical scenes throughout Scotland and England are included in this series. All of these postcards are the work of one man and always bear his name, Reginald Phillimore of North Berwick, about whom a great deal remains unknown.

Reginald Phillimore Phillimore was born into an upper middle class family on 23rd December 1855, near Manchester, England. He was the son of Dr. William Phillimore Phillimore, formerly Stiff, and Mary Elizabeth Phillimore Phillimore, née Watts. The family dropped the name Stiff which they did not like, and instead used their middle name twice. Dr. Phillimore was a medical practitioner at Nottingham Lunatic Asylum and held a position which gave him a place of honour and respect in the community.

His son Reginald was educated at a public school and Oxford University where he graduated B.A. He then entered into the field of education and took up a teaching post in a boarding school in Eccles, Lancashire. During his time as a teacher he continued his passion for art and made many sketches of the surrounding area which, years later, he used in his postcard series.

Although the 700 or more postcards he produced are predominantly of Scottish places and scenes, there can be found many famous cathedrals, castles and scenes of villages and towns throughout his native England.

In 1894 an event occurred that changed the whole direction of his life when his Scottish aunts left him 'Rockstowes', a Victorian villa at 9 Melbourne Road, North Berwick. From his studio there, through one of the large bay windows, he looked directly out to one of the most dramatic and beautiful scenes in Scotland, the magnificent Bass Rock. This amazing and awesome scene, and the town of North Berwick itself, became the inspiration for many of his unusual postcards. His move to Scotland, with its great wealth of beauty and history, also provided him with the impetus to use his talent and passion for these two subjects.

Phillimore's love for the view of the Bass Rock from his new home on the shore of the Firth of Forth never left him and it not only featured in many of his postcards but, on the reverse side of one of his cards of 'The Bass', he includes this advertisement: *Everyone should read 'The Bass Rock, its History and Romance' by R.P. Phillimore B.A. Price 1 Shilling.*

His postcards are not only charming illustrations but they contain many historical notes which add to the enjoyment and the education of both those who purchased his cards and those who received them.

In addition to expressing his passion for history and art, this shy and retiring man was an astute business man and was quick to recognise the great potential of postcards which had become so popular, at the turn of the century. He founded his own company to produce his drawings and this became a very successful commercial enterprise. It is because of this success that collectors today can still find his work for sale at postcard fairs.

His postcards were printed in black and white or sepia but many were hand coloured by a 14 year old girl from North Berwick, named Mary Pearson. One only needs to examine

Phillimore's cards to discover that this remarkable 14 year old became very skilled in her task, and had a pleasing and delicate sense of colour which added greatly to the appeal of Phillimore's work.

During my research among the citizens of North Berwick who remember Reginald Phillimore, I discovered an interesting fact concerning this artist. Scotland is famous for its 'Hogmanay' celebrations and Scottish shortbread, along with the world famous Scottish drink, is an important part of these celebrations. Brodie's Bakery, of 7-13 High Street, North Berwick, provided frosted shortbread rounds which were delivered to the artist's studio upon which he painted local scenes to order, and one of those featured most was that beautiful sight he looked out upon daily from his studio window, the Bass Rock. These beautifully painted shortbread rounds, which literally 'sold like hotcakes', were sent as gifts to relatives and friends throughout the world.

Many of Phillimore's postcards were printed in Berlin by the phototype or collotype printing process, a non-screen printing process, which produced a more sympathetic rendition of works of art and was particularly suited to his sketches. Today this process is still used for works of art and there is only one firm in Britain, Cowles of Ipswich, which produces works by this superior, although complicated process. On the reverse of Phillimore postcards can be found many variations of the name of his series including, 'The Phillimore Series North Berwick', R.P. Phillimore & Co., North Berwick, 'Phillimore Historical Series', Cathedrals, Abbeys, Churches, Castles, Towers etc., 'Phillimore Rustic Series' and even an impression made by a rubber stamp: 'R.P. Phillimore, Rockstowes, North Berwick.'

Although Phillimore produced most of his own postcards I have discovered one which has the imprint 'Phillimore' Series, Davies & Son Gloucester. There can be no doubt that this quiet, shy man was an astute business man who, when he moved to Scotland at the age of 39 to claim his inheritance of a beautiful villa situated on the shore of the Firth of Forth, was able to make his living through his greatest love: combining sketching with history. After a long life and an interesting career, in which he brought much pleasure and knowledge to people who sent or received his postcards, Reginald Phillimore Phillimore died at his beloved home 'Rockstowes' on 24th December 1941, only one day after his 86th birthday. He was interred in the family vault at Bridgnorth, Shropshire, on the River Severn near Wolverhampton. It is fitting that this man, who spent most of his life on the shores of the Firth of Forth in Scotland, should be laid to rest with his family in such a historical town that commands such a beautiful view of the River Severn 200 feet below.

Reginald Phillimore Phillimore, artist and historian, through his combined gifts, has brought a great deal of pleasure to many people through his series of delightful postcards. I am happy to be able to present a small sample of his work in this new book.

1. Quality Street, North Berwick, is featured in this drawing by Reginald Phillimore and was produced around the turn of the century. It was hand coloured by Mary Pearson, age 14, a local girl, whose work can be seen on many of Phillimore's cards. The street was so named because of the elegant houses which once lined both sides. In the background is Berwick Law, a large hill, and below it 'The Lodge', once the town house of the Dalrymple family, long associated with this community. Phillimore also includes the coat of arms of the Dalrymples which features, above it, the outline of Bass Rock owned by the family since 1701. In the 18th century, on the grounds of this house, was a well which was said to have curative and magical powers to improve ones beauty.

568 AIRSHIP SCOUTING OVER THE FORTH

R.E PHILLIM[...]

2. This is one of Phillimore's rarest drawings and shows an airship scouting the Forth over his favourite island of Bass Rock. This postcard was produced about the time of the First World War and a fleet of battleships can be seen behind the island. It may appear to be a scene from the artist's vivid imagination, but Phillimore certainly saw airships over the Forth and his town because East Fortune airfield, only 4 miles away, was an important airship station. On 2nd July 1919, airship R34, nicknamed 'Tiny' by her crew, made history when she successfully made the first non-stop transatlantic crossing by air, and on 6th July, after a flight of 108 hours and 12 minutes, landed at Mineola, New York. This epic crossing was acclaimed by banner headlines on the front pages of the world's newspapers of the time.

The Bass Rock, the last fortress that held out for King James, surrendered 1694 after a siege of 3 years

R.P.Phillimore

3. Bass Rock never fails to impress and Phillimore was impressed by his view of it from his studio window. He produced more of the Bass Rock than any other scene for his postcard business. Into this same scene of the volcanic plug, that was pushed up from the bottom of the sea millions of years ago, the artist drew historic details and events relevant to the area such as those illustrated on this postcard. A man-of-war fires on the castle that is holding out for King James but, after a siege of three years, the King surrendered, in 1694, when he was then taken to the Tower of London there to be held prisoner for 18 years. It is fascinating how Phillimore combines his skills as an artist together with his love of history to tell a story and to teach his spectators.

COAST GUARD STATION
& THE AULD KIRK : NORTH BERWICK.

KATE
WATSON

4. Just a few yards from the home of Reginald Phillimore are the old coast guard station and the ruins of the ancient church of St. Andrew, which dates back to the 12th century. The Celtic cross is a memorial to Kate Watson, a student of Glasgow School of Art, who on 27th July 1889, during a visit to North Berwick, lost her life while attempting to rescue a drowning boy. A bronze plaque on the cross is a memorial made to honour his classmate, Kate, by a fellow student of the Glasgow Art College and it tells the story of the brave young lady. Included on the memorial plaque is a portrait of Kate Watson which Phillimore illustrates on the lower left corner of his postcard.

The "NORMAN CLARK" to the Rescue: A ship in distress off NORTH BERWICK.
R.F. Phillimore

J. THORNBURN COXSWAIN

5. The local lifeboat used to be launched, on the beach, whenever a boat was in distress off the stormy and dangerous coast of North Berwick. Phillimore must have witnessed this scene many times and, in this drawing, he captures all the drama of this event when the lifeboat 'Norman Clark' is being launched in a heavy sea. This card, posted in the town in 1904, must have been produced about the time the 'Norman Clark' was new and had recently replaced the older 'Fergus Ferguson'. This was before an engine was fitted to the lifeboat and a large crew was needed to provide the manpower for the only means of propulsion, the oars. The coxswain, John Thornburn, a local fisherman whom Phillimore no doubt knew personally, served from 1892 until his death in 1914 and the artist honours him by drawing his portrait in the lower right corner.

FLIGHT OF AIRCRAFT OVER THE SEA. .570

R P PHILLIMORE NORTH BERWICK

6. There are two airfields within a 4 mile radius of North Berwick which were an important part of the defence of Scotland and the north of England in two world wars. One station was at East Fortune and the other at Drem. East Fortune, as well as fixed wing aircraft, had a fleet of airships often seen on lookout duties over the Forth and North Berwick. All that remains today at this airfield, are the ruins of the control tower, the officers' mess, which is now a part of East Fortune Hospital, where there is a bronze plaque to commemorate the world's first transatlantic crossing by the R34 airship, and an outstanding Museum of Flight which contains, among many interesting aircraft, relics from the R34. There is nothing in this rare drawing by Phillimore that he might not have seen many times from his studio window at 'Rockstowes'.

SWIMMING POND
NHS NORTH BERWICK No. 124 R.P.PHILLIMORE

7. The swimming pond at North Berwick is situated next to the old harbour, only a few hundred yards from the home of Phillimore, and there can be little doubt that he had many opportunities to observe the youth of the town, as well as adults and visitors, enjoying themselves there. When Phillimore made this sketch the pond was one of the finest along this coast. Today there have been many changes and the modernisation has included heating of the pool. Holiday-makers, young people as well as local people, still come in large numbers to enjoy the sea breezes, golf, swimming, wind surfing, and sailing along the coast at North Berwick. On the reverse of this card is a lovely vignette of the ruins of Waughton, near North Berwick, once the stronghold of the Ramsays and later of the Hepburns.

255   EAST BAY   NORTH BERWICK.

VIEW FROM EAST BAY.

8. This drawing of the East Bay, and below it the view looking out to sea, has been sketched in detail, like an architect's drawing, and Phillimore shows draftsman-like skills in his work. Dominating the scene is the ever present Berwick Law. Along the shore are these impressive Victorian villas, still standing today, but much changed since the early part of this century when the artist made his drawing. Berwick has always been a place for holiday-makers and many of these large villas were used as boarding houses for summer visitors. No doubt, this is how Phillimore saw East Bay when he first moved to the town and began his postcard publishing business.

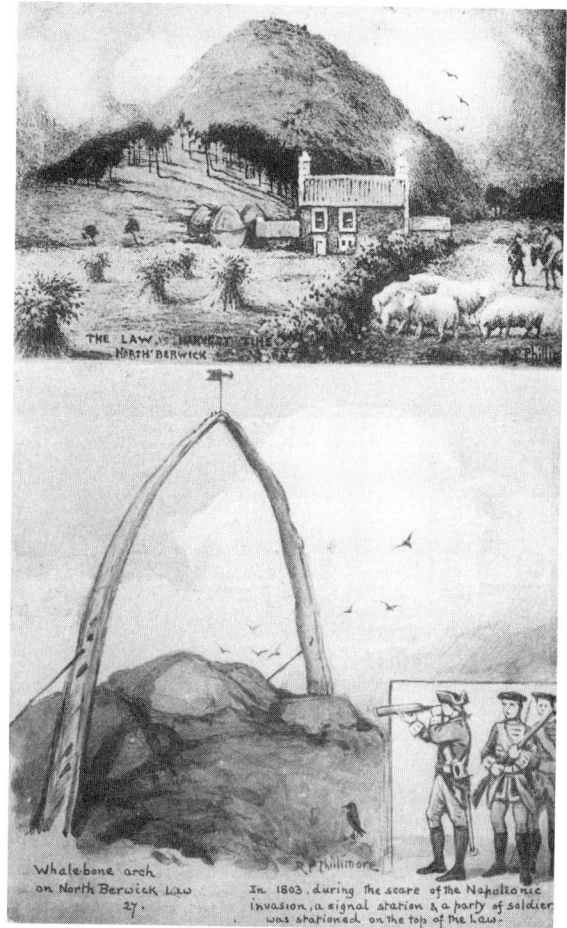

THE LAW NORTH BERWICK

Whalebone arch on North Berwick Law
27.

R.P. Phillimore

In 1803, during the scare of the Napoleonic invasion, a signal station & a party of soldiers was stationed on the top of the Law.

9. This postcard illustrates one of the dominant features of North Berwick and the history connected with it. Phillimore has drawn, on the top half of this postcard, Berwick Law, the hill that rises 613 feet above the town and the Firth of Forth. On the summit is an arch formed by the jaws of a whale and nearby there are ruins of a watch tower and signal station where a party of soldiers was stationed during the Napoleonic wars in 1803. The panoramic view from this vantage point is breathtaking and encompasses the entire Forth estuary to Edinburgh, the Kingdom of Fife and south to the English border.

Visited November, 1917.

L.H. 73

R. P. Phillimore.

*Off The Lamb
North Berwick
275.*

The SAILS WERE FILL'D AND FAIR THE LIGHT WINDS BLEW.

10. This is a postcard drawn from real life by Phillimore and was not the product of his imagination, as were so many of his historical cards. It is easy to see, by the set of the sails, that Phillimore is drawing this scene as he sees it. The picturesque fishing boat LH 73 is, along with the others, slowly drifting toward the harbour. Someone has written on the card that they visited here in November of 1917, but the card is of a much earlier date. Phillimore's work was always popular and was produced in large quantities, appearing in postcard racks years after its original production date. When Brown of the Mound, a famous Edinburgh stationer, closed relatively recently, boxes of Phillimore cards, in mint condition, were found in store.

NORTH BERWICK
FROM POINT CARRY.

11. When Phillimore's aunt left him her home in North Berwick she gave to him the chance to realise his ambition to earn his living as an artist. This profession flourished for him in the beautiful seaside town and he was proud of his achievements. When he passed away in 1941 he was remembered, not as the teacher, but as Reginald Phillimore, The Artist. North Berwick was a perfect setting for his second career. As this postcard shows, the town was a holiday resort and people came there to enjoy themselves by the seaside. Even to this day, boating from the harbour, swimming in the outdoor pool, and golf are just a few of the activities that draw holiday-makers to North Berwick. In the background can be seen Berwick Law, the hill that dominates the town. The Edwardian era Phil-limore portrays in his postcard has private bathing huts for changing, for these were the modest days, not like today, with a quick change into a bikini with a towel draped around the waist.

The Bass Rock Lighthouse and Ruins of Covenanters' Prison

R.P. Phillimore

In Prison on the Bass

Entrance to Fortress of the Bass

12. The style of Reginald Phillimore's drawing changed at different periods. This is one of his very early drawings and is more like a water-colour than a sketch. Sometimes his drawings are like the work of a draftsman with great detail, such as postcard Number 8 of East Bay at North Berwick. The date of posting on this card is 1909 but it was drawn much earlier, perhaps not long after this lighthouse was erected on ruins of the castle on Bass Rock, in 1902. Phillimore's card records that the fortress was used as a prison for covenanters. Today this island belongs to the Dalrymple family of North Berwick.

THE HARBOUR
NORTH BERWICK
R.P.Phillimore.

13. Reginald Phillimore's drawing of the small but lovely harbour gives something of the atmosphere of the place, around the turn of the century, when fishermen earned their living among the rocks and islands off North Berwick. Phillimore at this period was likely to see great steamships, such as the famous 'Fiery Cross', unloading day trippers who arrived in large numbers to see the sights of the town and to enjoy the golf, swimming and healthy air. These same ships then took on board passengers for cruises around Bass Rock for shooting or viewing the sea birds. They have always been in abundance on The Bass and it is believed to have the largest colony of solan geese in the world.

THE BASS ROCK
AT DAWN 381

R.P.Phillimore

"MILD RIDES THE MORN IN ORIENT BEAUTY DREST"

14. It is no wonder that Phillimore drew more pictures of Bass Rock than any other, because he looked at it every day of his life in North Berwick, and he saw it in all of its moods and conditions both by day or night, even at dawn, as in this postcard, Phillimore captures the beauty and grandeur of one of the most dramatic volcanic islands in the world. By adding his own quaint touches he makes it even more romantic. Anyone who has stood on the shore and looked over to Bass Rock can understand why Phillimore loved it and was fascinated by it.

Bombardment of Tantallon by General Monk

15. In this dramatic scene of Tantallon Castle, only 3 miles east of North Berwick, we have an excellent example of Phillimore's great love of history combined with his vivid imagination. Considered to be impregnable before the invention of gunpowder because it was protected on three sides by high sea cliffs and on the west side by two deep ditches and a drawbridge, it remained, for centuries, the stronghold of the proud Douglas family. It was indeed breached, after the invention of gunpowder, when Oliver Cromwell arrived in Scotland with his men. Under General George Monk the castle was reduced to ruins in a twelve day bombardment. To this day, standing high on the cliff above the Firth of Forth, the ruins of Tantallon Castle are a reminder of noble historical events that shaped the Scottish nation. This postcard was printed by the phototype process in Berlin.

Seal of William de Douglas 1332
Found at North Berwick 1788

R.P.PHILLIMORE.
NORTH BERWICK.

Covrt Yard
Tantallon Castle.
North
Berwick.
34

16. On his postcard of the court yard of Tantallon Castle Phillimore records an illustration of the seal of William de Douglas of 1332. The original seal was found in North Berwick in 1788. For centuries, all during the medieval period, this castle, so dramatic in its setting on a high cliff above the Firth of Forth, was the home of the Douglas family. It was not until the fifth Earl of Angus received it from James III that the long link to the Douglas family was broken. At the beginning of the 18th century Sir Hew Dalrymple purchased the castle and it eventually became a ruin, as it now stands today. On 30th October 1878 the castle again received Royalty when Queen Victoria arrived for a visit and was met by Sir Hew Dalrymple.

Text within the illustration: R.P.Phillimore · GALLANT DEFENCE BY BLACK AGNES AGAINST THE ENGLISH · SURRENDER TO EDWARD I · DUNBAR CASTLE NO. 221 · EDWARD ESCAPING AFTER BANNOCKBURN IN A FISHING BOAT · ST WILFRID IMPRISONED IN THE CASTLE BY KING EGFRID

17. Dunbar Castle, being in the border area of Scotland, saw much of the wars and border raids of invading armies. Here Phillimore illustrates all that is left of this once great castle which has been witness to some of Scotland's most turbulent history. After the assassination of Rizzio, at the Palace of Holyrood, Mary Queen of Scots left Edinburgh, at midnight, together with Darnley and took refuge in this castle. When Queen Mary left the castle and surrendered to the confederate soldiers on Carberry hill, near Musselburgh, Bothwell went to Dunbar castle but, afraid that he would be captured there, he fled by sea to Orkney. Phillimore refers to the defence of the castle against the English by the remarkable Black Agnes.

The village of Spott near Dunbar
R.P. Phillimore
THE VILLAGE OF SPOTT NEAR DUNBAR 285

18. This peaceful pastoral scene, drawn by Phillimore of the village of Spott near Dunbar, hides the true history of this area which figured in the Battle of Dunbar. General Leslie had his camp outside the village before he fought and lost the Battle with Cromwell. Many relics of the battle have been found, over the years, in the fields around Spott. There are also traces of an ancient camp to the south-west of the village which is thought to be Roman or Danish. In this area, early last century, belief in witchcraft was widespread and it was generally believed to have been the scene of the last witch-burning in Scotland. Such a small village had a notorious son, George Home, who was tried for the murder of Darnley. He then sat on the jury in the trial of Archibald Douglas for the same murder. Later he was assassinated by his son-in-law, James Douglas of Spott, one of the accomplices, in 1591, of the Earl of Bothwell, in the attempt against the King and Chancellor Maitland.

SCENE of the BATTLE of DUNBAR. THE BROXBURN AT BROXMOUTH. Sept 3 1650

19. The Broxburn or Spott Water at Broxmouth outside Dunbar was the scene of the famous Battle of Dunbar which took place on 3rd September 1650. This postcard is from the Phillimore Series and the artist includes two vignettes: one of Oliver Cromwell, the victor of the battle, and the other of fighting men in armour and on horseback against the inferior Scottish troops under the command of General Leslie, 1st Lord of Newark. He was later taken prisoner by Cromwell at Worchester and imprisoned in the Tower of London. The army of Covenanters led by David Leslie, who was fighting for Charles II, was defeated by Cromwell and the King had to flee for his life to the continent.

Labels within the illustration:

RUINS OF
St ADRIANS
MONASTERY
ISLE OF MAY
R.P.Phillimore

NEW LIGHT HOUSE.
3 MILLION CANDLE POWER
ISLE OF MAY.

PILOTS
SHELTER.

OLD LIGHT
HOUSE. 1636

MAY LIGHT 1636

20. This Phillimore postcard is the finest illustration of the old and new lighthouses on the Isle of May that I have ever seen and the artist includes several vignettes and historical notes of importance. On the bottom right is a small drawing of the first light tower in Scotland built in 1638. Phillimore incorrectly says 1636. Over 300 tons of coal from the Fife coal-fields were burned on this tower, yearly. The new lighthouse was completed in 1816 to the design of the famous Stevenson family, the lighthouse engineers of Edinburgh, and produced a light of 3 million candle power, guiding ships for almost two centuries into the Firth of Forth. In the left lower corner the artist has drawn the ruined cell of St. Adrian, a hermit, who came to evangelise the coast of Fife and was martyred on the Island by the Danes. In the middle ages this island became a place of pilgrimage and reputed miracles.

A Corner of Dirleton Village. Near North Berwick.

R.P. Phillimore. NORTH BERWICK

21. This peaceful scene of Dirleton village, by Phillimore, hides another more violent story. During the civil wars Dirleton, for a time, was occupied by Scottish guerillas called the moss-troopers. General Monk, on his march north, fought against them and a successful surrender was obtained of their leader, Captain Waite and two of his followers who were all executed. Dirleton Castle has also seen violent times throughout its long history since the 12th century. The village common was considered, last century, to be the finest coursing field in Scotland. Two thirds of the lands in this parish were owned by the Nisbet Ferguson family of Archiefield House.

Within the drawing:

DIRLETON CASTLE.
NORTH BERWICK.

On August 28th 1600 a Herald and Trumpeter
appeared at the gate of Dirleton Castle and
Summoned Earl Ruthven to appear before
King James I & Privy Council to answer
for his connection with the Gowrie Conspiracy.

R.P.Phillimore

RUTHVEN

22. In 1298 Dirleton Castle, owned by the Anglo-Norman family De Vaux, greatly harassed the march of the English army under Edward I. In retaliation it was besieged by Antony Beck, the martial Bishop of Durham, on behalf of King Edward to whom, after a brave defence, it surrendered. Phillimore captures the charm of this noble and graceful relic of the feudal ages in his drawing of it here. The castle is enclosed within a wall with a fine bowling green and a beautiful garden.

CONSULTING THE WIZARD AT TANTALLON CASTLE

DOUGLAS

321

R.P.Phillimore

23. The most remarkable feudal strongholds in East Lothian are those of the Douglases, the guardians of the main pass between the borders and the Lothians. Tantallon stands as a great ruin and reminder of the days when the Douglas family ruled this land. Phillimore looked from his home and could see this brooding ancient fortress and like the Bass Rock he made many drawings of it. This card makes reference to the Wizard of Tantallon Castle, one of the characters of a novel by Phillimore entitled 'The Wizard of Tantallon'.

FENTON TOWER KINGSTON Built in 1577 by Sir John Carmichael who took an important part in the raid of Reidsmire & was finally murdered by some English borderers

KINGSTON VILLAGE
HADDINGTONSHIRE. [242] R.P. Phillimore

24. Fenton Tower is another East Lothian ruin that appealed to Reginald Phillimore, who travelled with his sketch pad and drawing pencil through the area making drawings for his postcards. Here is another example of a castle being in the way of advancing armies from the south and suffering destruction because of it. Sir John Carmichael built it in 1577 and he too was murdered by English borderers. Nearby the ruined castle is the hamlet of Kingston which, in the middle of last century, had a post office and a population of 120.

ABERLADY CHURCH
AND LOUPIN'-ON-STANE
Dates from Norman times   No. 288
R P Phillimore.
Loupin-on

25. Aberlady is a pleasant village on the shore of the Firth of Forth and at one time, last century, was the harbour and bathing place for the town of Haddington, although this community is situated 4 miles inland. A church was built in the village in 1773, but the parish is much more ancient and belonged to the Bishop of Dunkeld. It is believed that the Culdees had a seat at, or near, Aberlady called Kilspindie and that name is preserved today by the local golf club. In front of the church stands the 'loupin'-on-stane', a mounting stone for the use of ladies and gentlemen, on horseback, arriving to attend services.

Within the illustration:

601

GENERAL COPE'S HOUSE
PORT SETON

Said to have been occupied by General Cope
the night before his defeat at Preston Pans 21 Sept 21st 1745

R.P. PHILLIMORE.

26. The Battle of Prestonpans, when the Scots, under Prince Charles Edward, won a famous victory over the English, under Sir John Cope, was fought on 21st September 1745. This house in Port Seaton, illustrated by Phillimore on his postcard, is said to have been occupied by Sir John Cope the night before his defeat. After the battle a marching song, 'Hey Johnnie Cope are ye still marching yet?' became popular with the troops. How fortunate that Phillimore included this sketch in his postcard series and has given to posterity a record of this building, for it no longer exists.

SALTCOATES CASTLE AND FARM : GULLANE.

R.P.Phillimore.

27. Unfortunately East Lothian was in the path of advancing armies from the south and many of its castles and abbeys were sacked, burned and looted. Today these ruins add to the romantic charm of the area and Phillimore captures that in his postcard series. There is nothing of great note about Saltcoates Castle near Gullane, nevertheless, it is a part of the history of East Lothian and, even as a ruin, it tells its own story. Many of these ancient ruins are as close to farm buildings as Saltcoates Castle is to this farm.

WHITE KIRK: celebrated on account of its Holy Well as a place of Pilgrimage in the Middle ages. NEAR NORTH BERWICK. Frequently visited by King James I.

RPPhillimore

Pilgrims going to WHITEKIRK

28. The original church at Whitekirk was probably founded in the 6th century by St. Baldred, the patron saint of East Lothian. A later church, dedicated to the Virgin Mary, became a place of pilgrimage from the 12th century until the Reformation and this church belonged to the monks of Holyrood. Both kings and queens came on pilgrimages to Whitekirk, including James I. The dowager-queen of James I, under the pretext of a pilgrimage, but for the purpose of performing a vow for the safety of her infant son, outwitted Chancellor Crichton and carried off her son, James II, in a chest to Stirling. Today, once each year, a pilgrimage walk from Whitekirk to Haddington is held in a spirit of ecumenical fellowship with both Roman Catholics and Protestants of all denominations taking part.

HADDINGTON
287 Birth Place of John Knox

JOHN KNOX

Phillimore

29. Haddington is an old East Lothian market town which, in the 12th century, was laid out as a long, narrow triangle, and these boundaries can be seen today by following the line of High Street, Market Street and Hardgate. Phillimore has not illustrated the grand part of Haddington but the outskirts of the town where the humble people lived, citizens like John Knox, who became the town's most famous priest and then minister.

THOMAS DE QUINCEY.
AFTER J·ARCHER·RSA

DE QUINCEY'S COTTAGE : LASSWADE. 419

R·P·Phillimore 1916

30. Thomas De Quincy, the author of 'The Confessions of an English Opium Eater' and an important contributor to Blackwood's Magazine, lived in Edinburgh from 1820 until his death in 1859, when he was interred in St. Cuthbert's Church cemetery. Many well-to-do Edinburgh citizens had summer homes in the country and De Quincey had such a cottage in Lasswade, which Phillimore illustrates in this postcard. He has romanticised the scene and has included his 'usual' flock of sheep for which he seems to have a fondness, but this adds rather than detracts from the charming drawing captures the once rural setting o Lasswade. It was here De Quincey placed his family, on his wife's death in 1834, while he himself lived in solitude, moving from one dingy lodging to another, struggling with opium which tragically had become a habit of a lifetime.

ROSLIN CASTLE AND ITS LEGEND.

Sir William St. Clair of Roslin wins his wager with King Robert Bruce that his two dogs "Help & Hold" would kill the deer before she could cross March Burn

31. The origins of Roslin Castle are obscure, but around 1100 William de St. Clair obtained from Malcolm Canmore much of the land of the Barony of Roslin and he probably erected the beginnings of the castle. In 1650 General Monk besieged the castle and destroyed much of it. Later, in 1681, a furious mob, chiefly tenants, plundered what was left of the castle. The legend that Phillimore refers to on his postcard concerns Sir William St. Clair, who won a bet with Robert the Bruce that his two dogs, 'Help and Hold', would kill a deer before she could cross March Burn.

Roslin Chapel 1851
"an unfinished thought in stone"

Founded by
WILLIAM St CLAIR
1446

R.P.Phillimore

"Seemed all on fire that chapel proud
Where Roslyn's chiefs uncoffined lie
Each baron for a sable shroud,
Each in his iron panoply."

SINCLAIR

32. Roslin Chapel was founded in 1446 by William St. Clair, Lord of Roslin and Earl of Orkney. Tradition says that he obtained the architectural design from artists in Rome. He was considerate of his craftsmen by providing good wages, housing, and a portion of land according to the ability they had displayed. This was 1446 and, because of this visionary attitude, the builder was able to obtain the finest of craftsmen. The building has many beautiful features and decorations and it prompted Britton, in his 'Architectural Antiquities of Great Britain', to say: 'This building is unique.' Phillimore has also here produced a skilful drawing for his 'Historical Series' of postcards.

The Phentice Pillar
Roslin Chapel.
Founded 1446
by William St Clair
R.P. Phillimore
101

33. The chief object of wonder in Roslin Chapel is this 'Apprentice Pillar', said to be the work of an apprentice during the absence of his master. Here Phillimore has made a delightful drawing of this pillar for his early postcard Number 101. The young apprentice stone mason has created a beautiful work of art, a mass of delicate and exquisite carving which never fails to inspire all who stand before it in wonder and amazement.

R.P.Phillimore North Berwick

BOWDEN CHURCH.
ONE OF THE OLDEST CHURCHES IN SCOTLAND

34. This night scene of Bowden Church has been included for two reasons. The village is very small and stands on the Hawick and Melrose road in Roxburghshire. There is no indication whether Bowden refers to the name of the church or the town. There is further confusion because Phillimore has included North Berwick, in larger letters than usual, on his card. He does tell us, however, that this is one of the oldest churches in Scotland. The second reason for including this card is to document the appeal of Phillimore's postcards. This card was sent in 1955, 14 years after his death, and although it is one of his latest productions, it is amazing that his work survived in postcard racks so long after his death.

LASSWADE 1554

R P PHILLIMORE NORTH BERWICK

WHEN THERE WAS NAE BRIG TO CROSS THE ESK RIVER.
ON JENEYS BRAID BACK THEY A'GAED THE GITHER.
FOR JENEY WAS HONEST, STOUT, SOBER, AND STEADY.
SHE CARRIED THE LAIRD, SHE CARRIED HIS LEDDY.
WHEN HE WAS RICHT SEATED THE DOGGIE FIRST GAED
THEN WAVING HIS STICK HE CRIED "JENNY" LASS, WADE.

THE LEGEND OF LASSWADE

35. Reginald Phillimore tells the legend of how Lasswade got its name. *When there was nae brig to cross the Esk River, on Jeney's braid back they A'gaed the gither. For Jeney was honest, stout, sober, and steady. She carried the Laird, she carried his Leddy when he was right seated. The doggie first gaed then waving his stick he cried 'Jenny' Lass, wade'*. But the more likely explanation of the unusual name for the village is from two words, *laeswe* and *weyde* which means a well watered pasture of common use. This is a good description of the site of this village.

Sir Walter Scotts Cottage, Lasswde. 301 R.P.Phillimore.

36. Lasswade was a pleasant rural place for summer houses and a place for convalescence for the wealthy citizens of Edinburgh. Phillimore illustrates the home of Sir Walter Scott which was his residence during some of the happiest years of his life. The village was also famous for the mills that were built along the River Esk which flows through it and they included four paper mills, two corn mills, an extensive gunpowder mill and a carpet factory. King George III especially liked Lasswade oatmeal and had a miller bring local oatmeal for the breakfast of his large family.

COTTAGE OF JOHN TOOD - THE "ROARING" SHEPHERD : SWANSTON. 416
knowing him by some sudden blast of bellowing. from far above me c'way oot amang the sheep"

37. The tiny hamlet of Swanston rests in a dell on the outskirts of Edinburgh at the foot of the Pentland Hills, and consists of a few cottages beside a burn. This rural place might well have been forgotten or become just another grouping of rural farm cottages, had it not been for the fact that the Stevenson family leased Swanston Cottage in the spring of 1867, and for the next 14 years they, together with their world-famous son Robert Louis, used it as a holiday home. In that same year Robert Louis Stevenson became an undergraduate in engineering at Edinburgh University, but three years later he changed, to the benefit of millions who have loved and admired his literary works, to study law and announced his intention to become a professional writer. Phillimore captures the rural and calm atmosphere in his drawing of the village.

38. This postcard illustrates the house and law office of Sir Walter Scott at 39 Castle Street, Edinburgh, and includes a portrait and the coat of arms of the famous son of 'Auld Reekie', who was born at College Wynd in 1771. He attended the Royal High School and Edinburgh University and later practised as an advocate from 1792 until 1806 and, in that year became Clerk to the Court of Session until two years before his death in 1832. It was as an author of romantic narrative poems, such as 'Marmion' and The Lady of the Lake, as well as historical novels, that Sir Walter Scott won world-wide fame for himself and created an international interest in Scotland that has since continued to this day. Phillimore has accurately drawn the author's house which has changed little to this day.

INCHKEITH
FIRTH
OF FORTH
322

R.P.Phillimore

39. Inchkeith is the most prominent island in the Firth of Forth and has a long history. I have visited the island many times in my yacht 'Kirsty Girl', and have explored the many ruins and tunnels some of which date back to Napoleonic times. There are also many relics left from the First and Second World Wars when men were stationed on the island to protect the fleet at Rosyth and the important link with the north, the Forth Railway Bridge. One interesting story about the island concernes King James IV. He chose a pair of orphans from Edinburgh and, as infants, sent them with a dumb nurse, to find out what was the natural language of man. A number of years later he discovered that language is learned through imitation and therefore his two orphans could not speak because their only companion was a nurse who herself could not utter a word. Phillimore has captured in his drawing the brooding clouds over the island and examples of the several kinds of ships that sail around the Forth.

LIGHTHOUSE INCHKEITH.   A.P.Phillimore

INCHKEITH FIRTH of FORTH

40. The majestic lighthouse on Inchkeith Island, three miles north from Edinburgh, out in the Forth, is a brownstone structure of architectural and historical note, built in 1804 by lighthouse engineer Thomas Smith. Only the summit where the lighthouse stands 70 metres above sea level, is clear of clutter. There remain ruins of an 1840 experimental light tower, gun emplacements, huge sheds, and underground tunnels left over from Napoleonic times and two world wars. Phillimore illustrates both the lighthouse and, below it, the island with several warships in the foreground, in this postcard of the later part of his career as artist, historian, and business man.

INCHCOLME MONASTERY
NEAR ABERDOUR '51

R P Phillimore

41. Reginald Phillimore sometimes used picture postcards already published as the basis for his drawings and this postcard proves it. His drawing of Inchcolm Monastery on the Isle of Inchcolm is almost identical to the postcard published around the turn of the century by John M. Logie, chemist of Aberdour. Phillimore even uses the same spelling of Inchcolm. The artist has added a sailboat, out in the Forth, and two men arriving on shore pulling up on the beach their row boat. Inchcolm is one of the most beautiful islands in the Forth and has a long association with Christianity in Scotland. It is believed that St. Columba landed here around 567, and David I was responsible for building the first abbey. During both world wars this island was fortified and manned to defend the Forth Railway Bridge. Today, rather than a place of religious pilgrimage, Inchcolm is a place for tourists and sightseers.

Within the illustration:

The CLIFFS
EARLSFERRY FIFE
340

MACDUFF'S CAVE
Here Macduff sought refuge from Macbeth
and was rescued by some fishermen, escaping
across the Forth in their boat. Out of gratitude
Macduff induced Malcolm Canmore to create
Earlsferry into a Royal Burgh.

MACDUFF
SAVED BY THE
FISHERMEN

R.P.Phillimore

42. The cliffs at Earlsferry form a break from the winds that sweep up and down the Forth, throughout the year, and create a protected beach which is a favourite with bathers even to this day. Earlsferry is an ancient Royal Burgh and received its charter from Malcolm III, between 1057 and 1093. It received its Royal status at the request of Macduff, who, in his flight from the vengeance of Macbeth, hid in a cave near this village. He was rescued by fishermen and transported across the Forth to safety at Dunbar. Out of gratitude Macduff asked Malcolm Canmore to create Earlsferry a Royal Burgh. Before 1154 Duncan, Earl of Fife, established a regular ferry service to Ferrygate, East Lothian, on the Archerfield estate near North Berwick, and this was used by pilgrims from the Lothians travelling to St. Andrew's, which had been a place of pilgrimage since a Greek monk brought the bones of St. Andrew to Scotland and deposited them in St. Andrew's Cathedral.

A favourite residence of Queen Mary

ROSYTH CASTLE & FORTH BRIDGE .300. R.P.Phillimore.

43. Here is another example of Phillimore using a picture postcard as the 'model' for his drawing. In the Reliable Series of postcards this scene is featured. The artist has added his own touches, however, such as the seagulls in flight, the sailing ship, and of course the lovely vignette of Mary Queen of Scots. This castle originally belonged to the Stuart family, but it eventually became the property of the Earl of Hopetoun. Sir Walter Scott, in his novel 'The Abbot', mentions Rosyth Castle and it was one of the favourite residences of Queen Mary. In the background can be seen the engineering wonder of last century, the Forth Railway Bridge, which celebrated in 1990 its centenary. This is a postcard from the 'Phillimore Historical Series' and has a distinctive drawing on the reverse side of two jousting knights on horseback.

HOLYROOD PALACE 1463   A HOUSE OF MANY MEMORIES   Phillimore

44. Holyrood Palace began as the monastery guest-house which stood near the Abbey Church. From time to time events of great importance brought here important guests, including the Kings of Scotland. By hosting such guests the Abbey of Holyroodhouse became a Royal residence. Phillimore calls it 'A House of Many Memories', none more memorable than those connected with the turbulent times of Mary Queen of Scots. Scotland's Royal residence is set in a natural city park, which is one of the most vividly striking and beautiful in the world.

Labels within the illustration:

LORD DARNLEY
LENNOX 1567.

CIPHER OF LORD DARNLEY
& QUEEN MARY.

LORD DARNLEY'S ROOM
HOLYROOD PALACE

418

R.P.Phillimore

45. Lord Henry Darnley was the weak cousin of Mary Queen of Scots and was four years her junior. Their marriage was fraught with problems and Mary was suspected of having him blown up in the Kirk o' Fields. Phillimore here illustrates the room of Darnley at the Palace of Holyrood.

506 &P.Phillimore

QUEEN MARY'S SUPPER ROOM·HOLYROOD.

It was in this room that the fatal supper party was held on the 9th March 1566. Into the recess of the window Rizzio retreated from the conspirators holding onto the Queen's dress, crying, "Giustizia! Giustizia! Sauve ma vie madame — sauve ma vie!" The first to strike a blow was George Douglas with the King's own daggar. Others dragged the poor bleeding creature through the bed-room to the door of the presence-chamber, where the conspirators, with fierce curses and yells completed their bloody work. Their victim was pierced by fifty six wounds.

PRIVATE STAIRCASE. up which the conspirators ascended.

46. Although this is one of the later postcards of Phillimore one would have to say that this is not one of his best drawings. Indeed his work as a historian surpasses that of the artist in this particular postcard. The drawing is of Queen Mary's small supper room at Holyrood Palace, where Rizzio was so brutally attacked and murdered. Phillimore records that Rizzio was stabbed 56 times. In the lower left corner is a sketch of the private staircase up which the conspirators ascended.

West Door   N° 61

HOLYROOD
      CHAPEL   FOUNDED BY KING DAVID I IN MEMORY
                      OF HIS MIRACULOUS PRESERVATION

FROM A STAG WHILST
HUNTING.

Phillimore

SEAL
OF
THE ABBEY

47. The quality of this drawing is much superior to that of Queen Mary's supper room, seen on the previous page. Phillimore has drawn a charming view of the west door of Holyrood Chapel and included a delightful vignette which tells the story of the founding of the Abbey, in 1128, by King David I. The King built the Abbey after his narrow escape from death by an enraged stag with the sudden appearance of a cross between himself and the enraged animal. It is from this incident that the area around the Palace of Holyrood, known as the Canongate, gets its coat of arms, which is a stag's head with a cross between its antlers. This can be seen in the seal of the Abbey drawn by Phillimore.

QUEEN MARYS BATH
EDINBURGH
over which Rizzios murderers
are said to have escaped.

MARY QUEEN OF SCOTS

48. This curious building stands today at the bottom of the Royal mile and, that it is ancient, there can be no doubt. Not a great deal is known about it, but it is usually referred to as the Bath House of Mary Queen of Scots. It could well have been such a building, but it is more likely to be just another small cottage in the grounds of Holyrood Palace near the Physic Gardens, the predecessor of the Royal Botanic Gardens, in Inverleith Row. The present location of Mary Queen of Scots' Bath House seems curious and unconnected to the Palace, but that is because of the building of the North Gate and a new roadway. Phillimore's drawing is a charming one, which captures the atmosphere of this ancient and curious building.

ST. GILES CATHEDRAL EDINBURGH

St. Giles a Greek hermit of the 6th century lived in the woods of the South of France subsisting on the fruits of the earth & the milk of a hind. This hind has ever been associated with St. Giles wits figure is to this day one of the supporters of the city Arms. To some Benedictine disciple from the south of France we doubtless owe the dedication of the Parish church of Edinburgh.

St. Giles

250

49. The Royal Mile, or High Street, just below Edinburgh Castle, is dominated by St. Giles, the premier Kirk of the Church of Scotland. It was built in the 14th and 15th centuries but altered during the Reformation. John Knox, the great Scottish Reformer, was minister at St. Giles until his death in 1572. This great firebrand of a preacher lies buried near the church. Phillimore has captured the atmosphere one could expect to find around the turn of the century and illustrates in his drawing the distinctive central tower, built in 1540, crowned by a lantern, supported by flying buttresses.

390
THE MARQUIS OF HUNTLY'S
HOUSE CANONGATE EDINBURGH:

R.P.Phillimore

The first Marquis of Huntly, George, is noted for having murdered the bonnie earl of Moray in 1591.
The second Marquis, a precise puritane, and therefore weill lyked in 'Edinburgh', perished at the block at the Cross of Edinburgh.
In 1753 the mansion was occupied by the Dowager Duchess of Gordon. A series of tablets adorns the front of the building containing the pious aphorisms usual in the 16th century.

50. From the drawing by Phillimore you can see that Huntly House, in the Canongate in Edinburgh, is made up of three smaller houses which were joined together in 1570. Phillimore records that George, first Marquis of Huntly, was noted for having murdered the bonnie Earl of Moray in 1591. The house was bought by the Incorporation of Hammermen who owned it until 1762. Today it is a wonderful museum of local history and must have been dear to the heart of historian Reginald Phillimore. On the reverse of this card, signed by Phillimore, is a lovely drawing of Edinburgh Castle, as it was before the Great Siege of 1573.

Summer House in the Garden where the Act of Union between the Two Kingdoms was signed.

372 MORAY HOUSE: CANONGATE EDINBURGH.

Erected by Ann Home Countess of Lauderdale in 1633. Became the property of her sister Countess of Moray in 1645 and remained in her family exactly 200 years. Cromwell stayed here on more than one occasion.

51. Moray House today is a distinguished College of Education on the High Street in the Canongate, Edinburgh, but at one time it was the residence of the Dowager Countess of Home, who had it built around 1628. It has connections with many historical events in the history of Scotland. In 1707 the Act of Union between Scotland and England was signed in a summer house in the garden. Oliver Cromwell was a visitor on a number of occasions, including a stay after the Battle of Dunbar in 1650. Among other distinguished guests was Charles I. It is said that while staying here in 1648, Cromwell revealed to the Covenanters that he planned to execute Charles I. In the mid-18th century the British Linen Company leased the house and installed weavers and spinners who worked from here for almost forty years. On the reverse of this postcard Phillimore has drawn 'The Blue Blanket', which is the Standard of the Incorporated Trades of Edinburgh.

GOLFER'S LAND, CANONGATE, EDINBURGH; Built by
a shoemaker John Paterson from the proceeds of a wager
won at golf from the Duke of York. On the gable is a coat of
arms with the appropriate crest of a hand holding a
golf club, and the motto "Sure and Farre".

R P Phillimore

52. Today Golfer's Land is known as Brown's Close and is at 65, North, the Canongate. Phillimore's drawing records a house that has an interesting story connected to it. Around 1681 the Duke of York, later to become King James VII, who was a keen golfer, made a bet with two English Lords on a game of golf. James chose as his partner a humble shoemaker named John Paterson, who was the best golfer in Edinburgh, and together they won the game. With his share of the wager, John Paterson built Golfer's Land and, to this day, there is a plaque there to commemorate the event and record the story. Above this plaque is a coat of arms which shows a hand holding a golf club over a helmet with the legend 'Far and Sure'. There is also an inscription in Latin which contains an anagram of John Paterson(e) which reads: 'I hate no person'.

Within the drawing:

646
OLD HOUSES IN THE COWGATE IS EDINBURGH. An ancient Author, Alesse wrote in 1530 that the nobility and chief senators of the city dwelt in the Cowgate and that none of the houses were mean or vulgar. It was originally known as the Sougate or South Street. Building here must have begun early in the 15 century.

PHILLIMORE'S HISTORICAL SERIES

53. On this postcard drawing of the old houses in the Cowgate, Edinburgh Phillimore has written 'Phillimore's Historical Series'. The artist made several series of cards and his 'Historical Series' is one of his largest. The Cowgate in the 15th century was the place where nobility and well-to-do professional people lived, and the houses in those days were considered 'genteel'. The Cowgate, at that time, was more likely known as Southgate or South Street. But all of that changed and the Cowgate became the place where the poor and destitute lived, crowded into tenement slums. It is not insignificant that the Salvation Army built their Hostel there and, as has always been their noble tradition, ministered among the poorest and most needy people of the city. Phillimore's drawing shows the Cowgate in the days when the poor lived there.

JOHN KNOX'S HOUSE, EDINBURGH.

NEATH THE WINDOW ARE THE WORDS ΘΕΟΣ — DEVS — GOD.
E STATUE AT THE CORNER, IS SUPPOSED TO REPRESENT
OSES RECEIVING THE LAW ON THE MOUNT. THERE MAY
LSO BE SEEN THE INSCRIPTION. "LUFE GOD ABUFE
L AND ZOUR NEICHBOUR AS ZOURSELF.
E INITIALS J·M AND M·A· ARE PROBABLY THOSE OF JOHN
OSSMAN AND HIS WIFE, TO WHOM THE HOUSE BELONGED IN KNOX'S TIME.

JOHN KNOX.

54. This 15th century house on the High Street is one of the great tourist attractions of Edinburgh, because it is believed to have been, at one time, the home of Scotland's greatest religious reformer, John Knox. But one of its early owners was a jeweller named James Mossman, Master of the Mint and Assayer to Mary Queen of Scots, whose father redesigned the Scottish Crown. Although James Mossman had the distinction of being jeweller to the Queen, he was later executed for having been one of her supporters. John Knox, elected Minister of St. Giles in 1559, was given use of the house as his Manse and, today, it is owned by the Church of Scotland as a memorial to the great Scottish reformer and the Reformation for which he was greatly responsible.

JOHN KNOX'S STUDY. 504
JOHN KNOX'S HOUSE · EDINBURGH ·

FROM A DRAWING
BY R P Phillimore

In 1561 the Magistrates ordered Dean of Guild to make
a warm study for Knox in the house, built of "bailles"
i.e. to be wainscotted or panelled. It may be that
in this study Knox composed the "Confession of
Faith" & the "First Book of Discipline" in which at

55. This is one of the few postcards by the artist that has written on it 'From a Drawing by R.P. Phillimore' and it is of John Knox's study in the John Knox House. No doubt Phillimore had made a larger drawing of the study for a customer and decided to use it also for his postcard publishing business. In 1561, the Magistrates of Edinburgh ordered the Dean of Guild to make a warm study for the great reformer. There can be no doubt that many of the writings of John Knox came from this room.

MERCAT·CROSS & CITY CHAMBERS·EDINBURGH.

R.P.Phillimore. 463

RESTORED BY MR GLADSTONE IN 1885.
ALL ROYAL PROCLAMATIONS ARE STILL MADE FROM THE CROSS.
HERE DARNLEY ASSERTED HIS INNOCENCE OF RIZZIOS MURDER &
BOTHWELL WAS ACCUSED AS THE MURDERER. CLOSE BY WERE
EXECUTED KIRKALDY OF GRANGE, THE ARGYLLS & MONTROSE.
IN 1692 IT WITNESSED THE BURNING OF THE SOLEMN LEAGUE & COVENANT

56. Here Phillimore illustrates the premier Mercat Cross in Scotland that stands in front of the City Chambers in Edinburgh. Most Scottish towns have their own Mercat Cross, where proclamations are made and memorial wreaths are laid, but it was also a place for public sales and purchase for the merchants of Edinburgh. In addition to these uses the Mercat Cross was a recognisable meeting place. This Cross was restored by Gladstone in 1885, but Royal Proclamations have been made from this place for centuries. It was also at this spot that Darnley professed his innocence of Rizzio's murder at Holyrood Palace, less than a mile away, and where Bothwell was accused of that same murder. Only a short distance away many were executed including the Argylls and Montrose. In 1692 the Solemn League and Covenant was burned near this spot. If this historic Mercat Cross could speak, it would be able to recall being witness to many of the historical events in the history of a great nation.

JENNY GEDDES STOOL
NOW IN THE ANTIQVARIAN MVSEVM

COVENANTS

ARCH BISHOP LAUD   KINGDOMS   CHARLES I

Sunday 21st July 1637 ranks as one of the memorable dates in Scottish History. It was on this day that the new Service Book was appointed to be read in St Giles. The two archbishops with several suffrigans, the Lords of Privy Council & the Lords of Session were present to give solemnity to the occasion. But when the Dean proceeded to read the service there arose such an uncouth noise & hubbub that not any one could either hear or be heard. It was in vain that Archbishop Spottiswoode endeavoured to allay the tumult and the service closed amid uproar and confusion. It was on this occasion that Jenny Geddes, an old woman who kept a green grocer's stall in the High Street is said to have flung the stool on which she had been sitting, at the Dean's head.

57. Phillimore produced this postcard to mark the event that happened when Charles I tried to introduce an Anglican service to Presbyterian Scotland. The King appointed a Bishop of Edinburgh and renamed the High Kirk of St. Giles to 'St. Giles' Cathedral', and presented a new order of service and prayer book. On Sunday, 21st July 1637 a large crowd, together with the town council and other distinguished guests, opposed to the King's changes to their church service, gathered for worship. When the Dean entered the pulpit and opened the new prayer book a shout was heard, 'Are ye sayin mass in ma lug?' upon which pandemonium broke out and a stool was thrown through the air and hit the cleric. Jenny Geddes, a cabbage seller on the High street, is credited by history with throwing the first stool which now rests in the Museum of Antiquities on Queen Street.

Within the illustration:

1745 ♥ TO THE KING

OLD WHITE HORSE INN
CANONGATE EDINBURGH.
Mentioned in Scotts 'Waverley'
as the resort of Prince Charles
Edward's cavaliers.' 244

R.P.PHILLIMORE

58. In White Horse Close, in the Canongate, was located the Royal Mews, but in 1623 Laurence Ord, a merchant of Edinburgh, built the White Horse inn and coaching stables. From the rear of this inn there left the coach for London, which, at this time, took over a week to arrive in the capital city. In 1745 the supporters of Bonnie Prince Charlie used this as their headquarters and drinking place. In 1793 William Dick, the founder of the Edinburgh Veterinary College commonly known today as the 'Dick Vet', was born in White Horse Close.

EDINBURGH CASTLE. 428.

I. PHILLIMORE

59. Hundreds of books have been written about Edinburgh Castle and one can understand the reason why, when you look at this drawing of one of the most beautiful settings in the world for a city. Phillimore includes on the reverse of his postcard his presentation of the castle from an ancient 1646 Dutch drawing. On this postcard can be seen the castle itself, which stands upon a huge volcanic rock and dominates the whole city. Below are the Princes Street Gardens and the National Art Gallery, which Phillimore often visited. There are few cities in the world that have a castle like Edinburgh and it is no wonder that Phillimore was inspired to include, in his postcard publications, one of his drawings of this magnificent sight.

Edinburgh Castle illustration, with inscriptions:

CAPTURE OF EDINBURGH CASTLE BY EARL RANDOL BY NIGHT ESCALAD 1313

EDINBURGH CASTLE.
Founded in 7th Century by King
Edwin of Northumbria
after whom the city is called:
Ceded to the Scots in 11th Century:
Afterwards held by King Edward I
Finally captured for Scotland
by Earl Randolf. A.D. 1313

R.P. Phillimore

60. This is a very special postcard by Phillimore, because it includes some interesting historical data and an unusual way of illustrating it in his drawing. The castle drawing is from the Grassmarket and shows some of the inns and houses in that quaint part of Edinburgh which has changed little even today. On the card is the drawing of the soldiers of the Earl of Randolf capturing the castle in 1313. The artist also records that the castle was founded in the 7th century by King Edwin of Northumbria, after whom the city is called. It was ceded to the Scots in the 11th century and afterwards held by King Edward I. It was finally captured for Scotland by the Earl of Randolf.

ARGYLL TOWER
EDINBURGH CASTLE

PORTCULLIS GATE FIRST
ERECTED BY DAVID II.
HERE THE TWO ARGYLLS
FATHER AND SON WERE
IMPRISONED PRIOR TO
EXECUTION IN 1661 AND
1685 RESPECTIVELY.

ARCHIBALD CAMPBELL
MARQUIS OF ARGYLL
EXECUTED 1661

ARCHIBALD CAMPBELL
MARQUIS OF ARGYLL
EXECUTED 1685

61. Edinburgh Castle is entered by Argyll Tower and Portcullis Gate, first erected by David II. It was here in the tower the two Argylls, father and son, were imprisoned prior to their executions in 1661 and 1685 respectively. The massive construction of this magnificent gate makes the entrance to Edinburgh Castle practically impregnable. Phillimore captures the strength of the tower in his drawing.

St Margaret's Chapel Edinburgh Castle Edward I received here the homage of the clergy of Scotland 1296

R.P.Phillimore

LANDING OF QUEEN MARGARET AT QUEENSFERRY AD 1067

62. In addition to drawing a delightful sketch of St. Margaret's Chapel at Edinburgh Castle, often thought today to be one of its oldest existing parts, Phillimore includes this information on the reverse of his drawing: 'Edwin the Saxon King of Northumbria built a fortress named after himself Eadwinesburh or Edinburgh on a rocky height near the Forth A.D. 617. He was the first Christian King in North Britain.' Queen Margaret is seen landing at Queensferry from her favourite home in Dunfermline. She was made a saint by the Roman Catholic Church and the small chapel that bears her name was built during the 11th century. Today near the tiny chapel is a small cemetery where dogs, used in military service, are buried.

MONS MEG, EDINBURGH CASTLE. [458]
Forged at MONS in 1476. Employed by James II at the siege of Thrieve Castle
when it is said to have carried away the hand of the Fair Maid of Galloway. In 1489 it
was used at the siege of Dumbarton and eight years later at the siege of Norham. In 168?
it burst on being fired in honour of the Duke of York. In 1745 it was removed to London
but in 1829 it was restored to Scotland through the exertions of Sir Walter Scott.

63. This famous cannon at Edinburgh Castle is known as Mons Meg and was forged at Mons, in 1476. At the time of its manufacture it was one of the largest cannons in the world and was used successfully in many battles until 1682, when it burst because of too large a charge as it was fired in honour of the Duke of York. For many years it was held in London, but as a result of the efforts of Sir Walter Scott it was returned to its rightful place at Edinburgh Castle in 1829. On the ramparts of the castle it has remained since then until recently when, to save it from the harsh elements of the north and thus preserve it for posterity, a special room in the castle was altered to house it indoors. When Phillimore made his drawing it was on the ramparts overlooking Princes Street.

Within the drawing:
EDINBURGH CASTLE
Ruins of the Well-house Tower, built in 1450.
Also Fountain of St Margaret, Queen of Scotland.

R.P.Phillimore
1911
430

64. Phillimore records the date, 1911, when he made the drawing for this postcard, something he seldom does. It gives the student of his work a key to the approximate dates of his other drawings, because he also records the number of this card which is 430. In this scene Phillimore has drawn the ruins of the well-house tower, which was built in 1450, a sight which is seldom seen today because it is hidden in Princes Street Gardens, although it can be seen from trains arriving at Waverley Station from Haymarket.

LADY STAIR'S HOUSE. EDINBURGH.
PHILLIMORE 482

Built in 1622 by Sir William Gray of Pittendrum. It was
occupied by The Dowager Lady Stair early in The 18th century.
Her Story was utilized by Scott in "My Aunt Margaret's
Mirror". It was restored by Lord Rosebery in 1907.
And opened by him as a museum Dec 5. 1913. 7

65. Lady Stair's House stands in the Lawnmarket in the Royal Mile and was built in 1622. It was the home of Elizabeth, Dowager Countess of Stair, after whom it was named. Lady Stair was a bright star in Edinburgh society although her husband, Viscount Primrose, was a man with a violent temper who abused his wife. An event in her life involving her husband and a fortune-teller was used as the basis for one of Sir Walter Scott's best short stories, 'My Aunt Margaret's Mirror'. By the time Phillimore made this drawing Lady Stair's house had undergone restoration, in 1907, by Lord Roseberry and had been opened by him as a museum, which purpose it still serves today.

AKERS
BOOTS
D&HEELED
LADIES
£ · /'5

191

49.5

R.P.PHILLIMORE

SHOEMAKERS LAND (BIBLE LAND)
CANONGATE EDINBURGH.
At the end of eighteenth century it was
the abode of a curious dwarf known
as Geordie Cranstoun. He figures twic
in Kay's remarkable Scottish portrait

GEORDIE CRANSTOUN
after Kay

66. Built in 1682, Shoemaker's Land in the Canongate was so named because it once contained the Hall of the Incorporation of Shoemakers. Next door was Bible Land, so called because of two quotations engraved on the building from Psalm 133 and Proverbs 20 verse 3. In this close lived Geordie Cranstoun, an Edinburgh character, who was a music teacher and is said to have been so small that when he was drunk, which was claimed to be often, he was put into a fishing creel and transported home to his mother by a porter. On one such occasion the porter balanced the creel and poor Geordie on the stair railings while he rang the door bell and, when reached over to retrieve the creel and poor drunk Geordie, he saw the creel and Geordie fall to his death in the basement below. Phillimore includes a small drawing of Geordie Cranstoun after the famous Edinburgh character painter, Kay.

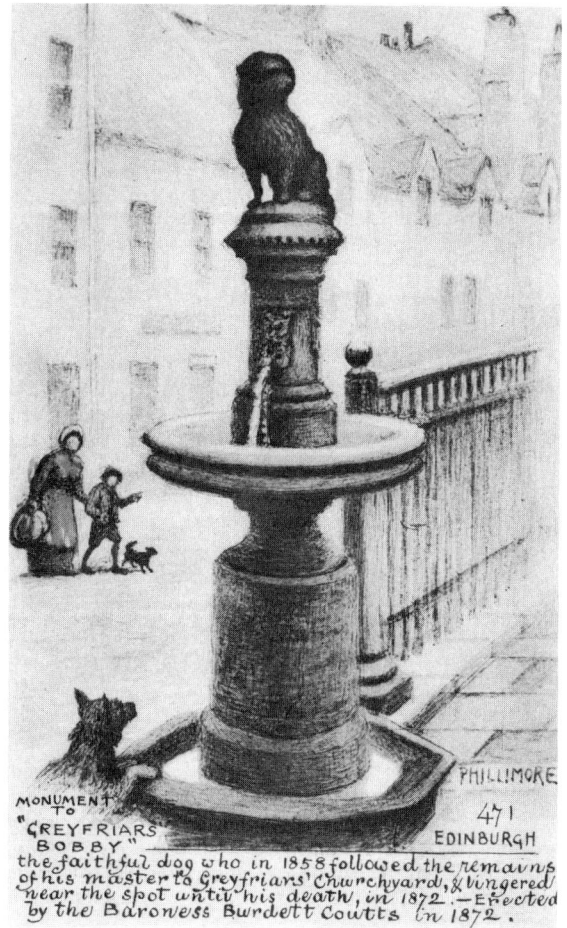

MONUMENT TO "GREYFRIARS BOBBY"
the faithful dog who in 1858 followed the remains
of his master to Greyfriars' Churchyard, & lingered
near the spot until his death, in 1872. — Erected
by the Baroness Burdett Coutts in 1872.

PHILLIMORE
471
EDINBURGH

67. One of the most delightful statues in all of Edinburgh is a monument to a dog called 'Greyfriars Bobby'. People from all over the world come to see the water fountain and memorial to a faithful dog who from 1858, until his own death in 1872, spent the rest of his life guarding the grave of his humble Master Jock. Baroness Burdett Coutts was so touched, as were many others including the Lord Provost of Edinburgh who gave Bobby the freedom of the city, that she erected this statue and drinking fountain for animals in memory of the faithful Bobby. To this day the loyal dog has captured the imagination of people all over the world. Books have been written about him and a famous Movie by Walt Disney was made and has been shown in cinemas throughout the world.

68. Sir Walter Scott made this house world famous by writing, in 1828, his historical novel 'The Fair Maid of Perth'. The heroine is the Fair Maid, whose actual name was Catherine Glover, the daughter of Simon Glover, who lived in the Curfew Row area of Perth. The house illustrated by Phillimore in this postcard stands on the site of Simon Glover's house and, although it does not date back to the setting of the great novelist's thrilling story in the 14th century, records in Perth can trace back to the history of the site. In the lower left corner of the postcard Phillimore has drawn a portrait of the Fair Maid.

UCALD STEWART

NELSON

CARLTON HILL EDINBURGH. 462 PHILLIMORE
ROYAL OBSERVATORY; DUGALD STEWART & NELSON MONUMENTS.

69. Second only to Edinburgh Castle Calton Hill commands the attention of those who view the skyline of 'Auld Reekie'. In the left upper corner of Phillimore's drawing is Lord Nelson's monument, a tower in the form of a telescope to honour the great naval hero. In the centre left is the philosopher Dugald Stewart's Memorial and the first Royal Observatory. However, it is not so much what can be seen on Calton Hill, but rather what can be seen from it, that gives it its popularity with visitors. From this vantage point can be seen some of the most beautiful vistas in the world from Arthur's Seat and Salisbury Craig to Edinburgh Castle and across to the Kingdom of Fife and down the Firth of Forth to the North Sea. The view from this vantage point down Princes Street is considered by many visitors to Edinburgh to be one of the most scenic to be viewed in any capital city.

70. This beautiful building was first known as Heriot's Hospital because it was used for that purpose for Cromwell's wounded soldiers. Today it is known as Heriot's School and was the gift of George Heriot, Edinburgh banker and jeweller to James VI, for the needy children of Edinburgh burgesses. It is interesting to note that, in 1787, the gardens of this school were used by the Italian balloonist, Vincenzo Lundardi, when he made his ascent over the Firth of Forth. Many famous pupils attended Heriots but none more famous than an orphan who came to the school in 1764 and later became one of Scotland's greatest portrait painters, Sir Henry Raeburn.

THE FLODDEN WALL
THE VENNEL EDINBURGH.

369

This fragment of the ancient wall runs from
Lauriston to the Grassmarket. It was
hastily erected by the citizens of Edinburgh
in 1513 after the disastrous battle of Flodden
in which the gallant King James lost his
life and many Scottish nobles perished.

A very interesting account of King James
and a thrilling description of the battle
of Flodden may be read in the Historical
novel "The Wizard of Tantallon". Price 6d

R.P.Phillimore

KING JAMES IV

R.P.Phillimore & Co. North Berwick

71. This fragment of the wall which once surrounded ancient Edinburgh, running along the Vennel from Lauriston to the Grassmarket, is called Flodden Wall, because the citizens of Edinburgh in 1513 erected it after the disastrous battle of Flodden in which their King James lost his life. Phillimore the artist advertises Phillimore the historian, when on his own postcard he writes: 'A very interesting account of King James and a thrilling description of the battle of Flodden may be read in the Historical novel, "The Wizard of Tantallon". Price 6d R.P. Phillimore & Co. North Berwick.'

DRYBURGH ABBEY – FROM EAST. 442.

R.?Phillim

ANSELM, the Apostle   GREGORY, the Ecclesiastic   JEROME, The Reformer
Preaching friars from old Melrose visit Dryburgh.

72. In Sir Walter Scott country in the borders of Scotland is this ancient ruin known as Dryburgh Abbey, which was founded by David I in 1150. Like so many of the abbeys in the border towns of Scotland it was sacked and burned several times by the English during their Border raids. In the 16th century it was left to decay and today remains a ruin but also a place of pilgrimage for lovers of the writings of Sir Walter Scott, who is buried in St. Mary's Aisle in the ruins of the abbey. Another famous son of Scotland, Field Marshal Haig, the British Army's Commander-in-Chief in the First World War, is also buried in the abbey. Phillimore includes a small drawing of Friars from nearby Melrose Abbey, visiting Dryburgh.

Text within the image:
BATTLE of BANNOCKBURN
AD . 1314

R P Phillimore

ROBERT BRUCE

LAY THE PROUD USURPERS LOW
TYRANTS FALL IN EVERY FOE
LIBERTY IN EVERY BLOW
LET US DO OR DIE

73. Stirling Castle was the Scottish Royal Palace until 1603, when James VI became the King of England. It stands on solid rock overlooking the beautiful Forth Valley. Phillimore includes in this postcard of the castle reference to one of Scotland's greatest victories when, in 1314, Robert the Bruce in the Battle of Bannockburn, which took place within 3 miles of the castle, defeated the English army which was three times larger than his own. This postcard was printed in Berlin for the Phillimore Series.

BURNS COTTAGE.
108
P.P.PHILLIMORE.

74. The Plough-boy Poet, Robert Burns, one of Scotland's greatest literary sons, was born in this cottage in Alloway which Phillimore drew for his postcard. The artist has captured the calm and rural setting in Ayrshire that this cottage enjoyed at the time the drawing was made around the turn of the century. Today all has been sanitized, cleaned up as it were, for the tourists and Burns lovers who flock here in the thousands on foot, by car and in bus parties, to worship at the shrine. Burns' own background, however, was different. He was poor and claimed himself that he was born to the plough, although he found solace in literature and the lassies. At 28 he was the toast of Edinburgh society, but he never did fit in. Nine years later he died, and while he was being buried, his last child was being born.

75. Phillimore travelled throughout Britain to make the drawings for his postcard business. Here can be seen his drawing of Blair Castle in Perthshire, the ancestral home of the Duke of Atholl whose ancestor, the first Duke, was its builder in 1269. Phillimore has perfectly captured the magnificent Highland scenery in this early postcard sketch.

CASTLE
BRIDGNORTH
Built 1102 by Earl Robert
de Belesme. Destroyed 1649

R.P.Phillimore

1649 Siege of Bridgnorth Castle
Bombardment from Pampudding hill

76. Although Reginald Phillimore was an Englishman, most of the postcards in this book are from Scotland and, in particular, the area around Edinburgh and North Berwick. When his Scottish aunts left him a home in North Berwick his career as an artist and historian began and it was there that he established his postcard business. When he died in December 1941, however, his body was brought back to his home in Bridgnorth, the ancient market town on the banks of the Severn in Shropshire, to be interred in the family vault. This last postcard Phillimore made of his home town with the ruins of the 12th century castle, illustrated in the upper half, and its siege and destruction, in 1649, below. From the beautiful view out to sea to the Bass Rock to the high cliffs above the picturesque Severn, Reginald Phillimore returned to his birthplace for the last time for peace and rest.